Money and Trade in Our Nation

Shelly Buchanan, M.S.Ed.

Consultants

Shelley Scudder
Gifted Education Teacher
Broward County Schools

Caryn Williams, M.S.Ed.
Madison County Schools
Huntsville, AL

Publishing Credits

Conni Medina, *M.A.Ed., Managing Editor*
Lee Aucoin, *Creative Director*
Torrey Maloof, *Editor*
Marissa Rodriguez, *Designer*
Stephanie Reid, *Photo Editor*
Rachelle Cracchiolo, *M.S.Ed., Publisher*

Image Credits: Cover, pp.1, 12, 24–25
Getty Images; p.16–17 Norbert Michalke/AGE
Fotostock; p.19 Erik Isakson/AGE Fotostock; p.4
Alamy; pp.28, 29 (bottom) Associated Press; pp.9,
11, 27, 32 iStockphoto; p.10 Library of Congress
[LC-USZ62-41874]; p.14 Library of Congress
[LC-USF33-011056-M1]; p.18 Library of Congress
[LC-DIG-ppmsca-19044]; p.23 Library of Congress
[LC-USZ62-95653]; p.20, p.24–25 Newscom;
All other images from Shutterstock.

Teacher Created Materials

5301 Oceanus Drive
Huntington Beach, CA 92649-1030
http://www.tcmpub.com
ISBN 978-1-4333-7001-4
© 2014 Teacher Created Materials, Inc.

Table of Contents

This girl trades money for clothes.

What Is Trade?

Trade is a word you hear a lot of people use. You may hear your teachers or parents use it. News reporters use it, too. It is an important part of our nation.

This is a one-dollar bill.

Dollars and Cents

Long ago in the United States, each state used different money. Today, all states use the same money.

Trade is when people buy, sell, or swap things. The system of trade and money in our nation is called the **economy** (ih-KON-uh-mee). The economy is the way people use money to make, buy, and sell things.

The economy is also about **resources** (REE-sohrs-ez). Resources are things that a nation has and can use to make money. People use resources to make things to sell. Natural resources are materials found in nature. Water, oil, and wood are natural resources.

This waterwheel is using water as a natural resource.

Some of these resources are unlimited. Water and air are always there. But other resources are limited. This means they can run out. Oil and wood are limited. So, people should plant a new tree if they cut one down.

This is an oil pump. Oil is a limited natural resource.

Trade helps people get what they need and want. *Needs* are things we must have to live, such as food, clothes, and homes. *Wants* are things we do not need but would like to have, such as toys, music, and games.

These people are buying food in 1942.

It is important to buy things we need before buying things we want. We do not always get the things we want. Can you think of other examples of needs and wants?

Toys are fun, but we do not need them to live.

Producers and Consumers

It takes many people to make trade and the economy work. Both **producers** and **consumers** are needed. Producers use resources to make goods, or things. These goods are also called *products*. Producers then sell their goods. People who buy these goods are called *consumers*.

These women are producing shoes.

Producers also provide services. A *service* is work or help that is for sale. A plumber (PLUHM-er) who fixes a sink is providing a service. The plumber is a producer. The person who pays the plumber for the service is the consumer.

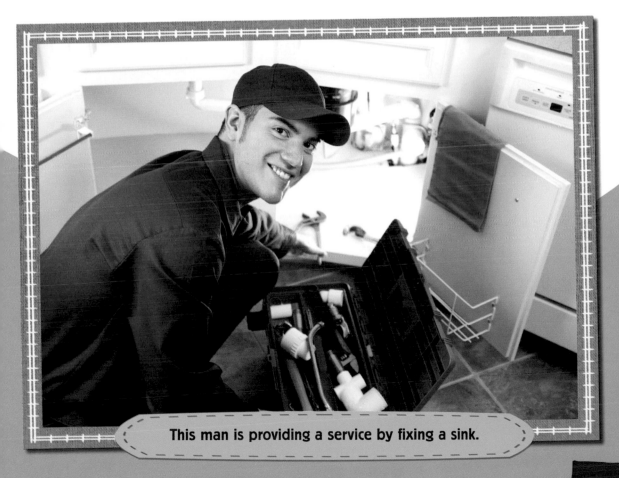

This man is providing a service by fixing a sink.

We are all producers and consumers. Think of the goods and services you use. Do you ever buy books or get a haircut? That makes you a consumer because you are using money to buy goods and services.

These kids buy soda in 1950.

Do you make money for doing chores around your home? That makes you a producer because chores are services. Can you think of any other ways you act as a consumer or a producer?

These people are shopping online.

Working Together

We depend on one another to get what we need and want. If we do not have the resources to make something ourselves, we can trade with one another.

This farmer grows corn in 1936.

Some foods, like corn, do not grow well in certain parts of our country. Corn grows better in states like Iowa (AHY-uh-wuh). So, people living in a different state may buy corn that is grown in Iowa. This way, we can all enjoy the same kinds of food. We can get what we want and need.

Why Iowa?

Corn grows well in Iowa because the state gets lots of rain. It also has the rich soil that corn needs to grow.

This is a field of corn.

The demand for these boots is low, so they are on sale.

Supply and Demand

Supply is how much of a good or service there is to sell. **Demand** is how many people want to buy that good or service. Supply and demand set the price for goods and services. The price is how much something costs.

Demand goes up when we buy things.

If there is a lot of one good and only a few people want it, then the price will be low. That good may even go on sale. This means that it is sold at a lower price. But if there is a small number of one good and a lot of people want it, then the price will be high.

Boom or Bust?

Sometimes the economy is strong. This means that there is a high demand for goods and services. To meet that demand, producers sell lots of goods and services. They earn money. Then, they use that money to buy other goods and services.

These people are buying and selling goods in New York City in 1901.

Most people make money in a strong economy. There are many jobs and a lot of trading.

This man produces and sells food.

These men cannot find jobs. They are waiting to get a nickel from a church in the 1930s.

Sometimes, the economy is weak. This means that the demand for goods and services is low. Stores can go out of business or close down. People may lose their jobs. Sometimes, they cannot find new ones. This is a problem for the economy.

When demand is low, some stores go out of business.

When people cannot work, they cannot earn money. This means that they cannot buy things. They have no money to spend on goods and services. Producers then lose money.

The economy runs in **cycles**. This means that the economy goes back and forth between being strong and being weak. When the economy is strong, it is called a *boom period*. This is when many people are working. They make and spend money on things they want and need.

People have more money to buy things in boom periods.

Then comes a *bust period*. This is when the economy slows down. It becomes weak. People lose their jobs and do not make money. There is less trading of goods and services.

This mother loses her job in a bust period in 1936.

A **government** (GUHV-ern-muhnt) is made up of a nation's leaders. Our government tries to make the economy strong. It makes sure people trade fairly. It also tries to help people make money. It does this by making jobs for people. Building roads and cleaning parks give people jobs. These jobs also help the community (kuh-MYOO-ni-tee).

These men are working for the government in 1934.

The government pays for the jobs with **taxes**. Taxes are money that people pay to the government. This money then pays for things like roads and schools.

These government workers are paving a road.

Money, Trade, and You

You are part of trade in our nation. You are a producer and a consumer. You and your family pay for goods and services. You provide services in your home or community. You may wash the dishes or walk a neighbor's dog.

This boy walks his neighbor's dog.

When you grow up, you will have a job. You will make money and pay taxes. How will you make and spend your money? What part will you play in our nation's economy?

This girl wants to be a doctor when she grows up.

Learn It!

Ask an adult to help you meet a worker in your community. Ask the worker about his or her job. Find out what goods or services he or she provides.

This girl is talking to a police officer.

This boy is helping a veterinarian.

This girl is meeting a firefighter.

Glossary

consumers—people who buy goods or services

cycles—a set of events that happen again and again in the same order

demand—the need to buy goods and services

economy—the system of goods and services being made, bought, and sold in a country

government—a group of leaders who make choices for a country

producers—people who make goods or provide services

resources—things a country has and can use to make money

supply—the amount of goods and services for sale

taxes—money that a government makes people pay

trade—to buy, sell, or swap goods and services

Index

Your Turn!

Needs and Wants

The kids in this photo are playing with toys. Toys are wants because you do not need them to live. What are some things you need? What are some things you want? Make a list of each. Share the lists with your friends or family members.